This story is about a young boy named David who is an only child. David seems to pick questionable kids at times to be his friends.

Often, his mother Joanne tells him to be patient and good friends will come in time. Since David was an only child, he felt that if he follows his mother's advice, it would take forever to find friends. Because in his mind, he has a lot of playing to do and he needed to get busy because he said he's not getting any younger.

So, David started his quest for finding friends as soon as possible. David was so excited that he dismissed what his mother said, as if she did not say anything at all.

QUESTION:

Do you think David had a bright idea by not following his mother's advice?

Do you remember what David forgot to do in his pursuit to find friends? Hint: it's something to do with what his mother said.

David was in the backyard playing basketball by himself and he saw two boys crossing the street around the corner from his house. This was the first time he saw them. He was so excited about making friends that he forgot to tell them his name and ask them their names. David invited the two boys over his house right away to play basketball with him.

The boys went over to David's house to play basketball. Everything was going well and they appeared to be having fun.

Ten minutes into the game, something happened! The boys ran away with David's basketball. David stood there with his mouth wide open. His mouth was so wide, flies could have flown into it.

David was upset about what happened to him, so he made a vow to himself not to tell his mother.

Hmmm. . . David acts like a leaping frog; he leaps before he knows where he's going to land. In David's case, he was moving too fast to make friends.

In this picture, circle the place you think the frog will land.

Turn the page to see how David is doing with his newfound friends.

What would you have done different if you were David?

David finally made a friend at school and his name was Jackson. He only knew Jackson for two days and not enough time to call him a friend. But David called Jackson his friend anyway because Jackson was always nice to him.

Turn the page to learn something about Jackson. . .

Jackson had a tiny secret that he kept to himself. Jackson loved practicing his karate on kids that were smaller than him. He was considered a secret bully. He was in this gang called Crush the Smaller Kids After School. Jackson is going to ask David to join the gang on Thursday.

Turn the page. . .

On Wednesday, David was walking home from school and saw a large crowd of small kids being bullied by the older and larger kids. Then he saw his friend Jackson in the middle of everything.

David was shocked and disappointed because he made a bad choice for making Jackson a friend without getting to know him first.

Jackson spotted David glancing over at him and knew from the look of disapproval on David's face that David wanted no part of what he was involved with. There was no reason for asking David anything on Thursday. From the look in David's eyes, Jackson knew their friendship was over. David's disapproval challenged Jackson to rethink his position on being a bully. No one ever caused him to feel that way.

David realizes the friends he chose were not good choices. Their personal values were not like his. David told his mother about everything and said he was sorry for not following her advice, and that he loved her.

Now David has good friends and their friendship is growing with time.

Things to ponder on when you are on your friendship journey:

1. Sometimes our parents might know a little something-something to help us on our journey.
2. It takes time for friendships to grow.
3. Get to know people who you want to be friends with.
4. Be patient.
5. Friends must be trustworthy.
6. Friends must be dependable.

Can you think of some things that you like to see in a friend when you are on your friendship journey?

Please write them below:

List what you like to see in finding good friends:

1.
2.
3.
4.
5.
6.

On this page, draw a picture of you and your best friend in the middle:

On this page, draw a picture of you and your best friend in the middle:

www.ingramcontent.com/pod-product-compliance
Ingram Content Group UK Ltd.
Pitfield, Milton Keynes, MK11 3LW, UK
UKHW061314070826
14089UKWH00047B/214
9798218468057